Social Media for Restaurants

KEN TUCKER

With Insights from

Nina Radetich

Social Media Marketing for Restaurants

opinion, and are not intended to malign any religion, ethnic group, club, organization, company, individual or anyone or anything.

Although we make strong efforts to make sure our information is accurate, Ken Tucker and Nina Radetich cannot guarantee that all the information in this eBook is always correct, complete, or up-to-date.

ISBN-10: 197628998X
ISBN-13: 978-1976289989

Foreword

Thoughts on using this book

Many of you reading this book may already be using social media for your restaurants. You might be reading this book to find a way to gain a competitive advantage over competitors and to grow your business.

So, first off – congratulations. A commitment to life-long learning is the hallmark of any truly committed entrepreneur.

But here's the thing – don't let every shiny new object in the world of online marketing distract you from your primary goal – get more customer and build the brand of your restaurant.

There is so much information available today than time to consume it. Social media platforms are constantly changing their features and capabilities. And occasionally, a major new platform becomes popular and warrants consideration.

This book provides an excellent overview of what social media platforms and local search related sites are, and how you can use them for your restaurant.

I know the authors of this book personally and have seen their work first-hand. They not only consistently deliver results for their clients; both have been very generous in sharing their knowledge by way of training fellow members of the Duct Tape Marketing Consultant Network. I think this speaks volumes because it allows me to confidently assure you that you are about to read some pretty good stuff.

Ken Tucker and Nina Radetich are rock star marketing professionals in the Duct Tape Marketing Consultant Network. As certified marketing consultants they:

- Have completed my intensive training program;
- Participate in ongoing marketing training and mentoring;
- Have exclusive access to an arsenal of proven tools and methodologies;
- Are members of an elite, fast-growing global network of talented small business marketing consultants;
- Are certified to install the Duct Tape Marketing System.

At Duct Tape Marketing, we teach that strategy before tactics is the key to creating a winning, high ROI marketing plan. Getting your strategy right from the get-go is the only way to create a web-centric, inbound marketing platform that will consistently draw ideal customers to your doorstep.

Once you get the right strategy in place, however, tactical execution is the only way to ensure that your marketing plan will produce results.

This eBook is broken into chunks, and in a practical, easy-to-read format. Each chapter focuses on a social media platform that has been demonstrated to be effective in helping restaurants grow and retain customers. This eBook will give you - the business owner, restaurant manager, or social media manager - the education you need to understand and apply important tactics to your restaurant.

I highly recommend this eBook and apply what you learn. There is no question your business will generate more business and more leads. Period.

John Jantsch
Author of Duct Tape Marketing
www.DuctTapeMarketing.com

CONTENTS

1 INTRODUCTION

Why is Social Media so Important for Restaurants?

When it comes to using social media for restaurants there are a couple of things that immediately come to mind. First, people love to share their experiences when they're out with their friends or their family. It's become a pretty natural thing for people to take pictures of their food and post them on Facebook. Many are writing reviews on Facebook or Yelp. From that perspective, it's very important.

Second is the idea of social proof. There's a great non-digital analogy. When we drive past a busy restaurant and we see people standing in line waiting outside the door, that catches our attention. Then we look across the street at another restaurant and there's nobody standing in line.

We want to go to the busy crowded restaurant because we see a lot of people there and they're willing to stand in line and wait for that experience. If people are willing to do that, it sends a signal to us that it's something we might want to experience. That whole concept is considered to be social proof.

The same thing comes into play on social media in a really powerful way. Social proof happens when people see that there are a lot of Facebook page likes, a lot of comments, a lot of shares of a particular post on Facebook, or a lot of Twitter likes or re-tweets. When this engagement happens, it gives a psychological clue to the person who's viewing those posts that this must be important. And if engagement comes from one of their friends or acquaintances, or from somebody they trust, then it sways their opinion.

Social proof actually moves people into a different stage of the buying cycle. If they were just aware of a particular restaurant, now all of a sudden they're interested in going to that restaurant. Seeing a post on social media might even sway someone's decision on where they decide to eat that day.

When it comes to social proof, people post about their experiences for a variety of reasons. They are genuinely sharing a great experience, they want to be seen as a person in the know, or they are posting because they want to show off where they've been. Regardless of the motivation behind why people share, if their experience is positive it is great for the restaurant.

What Social Media Sites Should a Restaurant Consider?

When it comes to using social media for restaurants, I think you have to consider Facebook, Instagram, Google My Business, Yelp, Twitter, Foursquare, Pinterest and Snapchat.

The 800 pound gorilla in the room is Facebook. If you only have the ability to focus on one social media site, Facebook is the one to use. Facebook has a really strong user base across age groups and demographics so using Facebook will help you reach your target audience pretty effectively.

I really like Twitter because I think Twitter is a marketing powerhouse. It gives you the capability to find fantastic opportunities to engage new customers or to find current trends. Twitter allows you to see what people are saying and what your competitors are doing which makes Twitter very important.

Yelp is extremely important for restaurants. Yelp was created to be a user review site. Users started going in and posting reviews of their favorite restaurants, coffee shops, and bars. It's become one of the most influential review sites on the internet.

Yelp is also a fantastic source for driving traffic to your website. When people use the Yelp app, restaurants and other businesses are found by shortcutting the typical Google search. If your restaurant is not listed on Yelp or it is incorrectly listed, people using the Yelp app won't find you, and you're going to miss an opportunity to attract new customers. Having your restaurant accurately and positively listed is kind of like a pipeline right to your business with Yelp users.

There are many other apps that might make sense for a restaurant like OpenTable or TripAdvisor, but Yelp is really important because of the prominence it has in local search results – typically ranking near the top of the first page.

Foursquare is a fun site and it's really heavily driven based on an App that you download on your Smartphone. What you do with Foursquare, as a user, is check in (through a sister app, Swarm) and when you check in you have the opportunity to earn stickers and find friends nearby.

What's really fantastic about Foursquare for business is that they give you the ability at no cost to create specials that show up on your business listing as well as when someone is searching for specials nearby. The user can redeem the special by simply showing their phone.

You claim your Foursquare listing so you can create

these specials and keep your business listing up to date including your website, your hours of operation, and your phone number.

Google My Business has become SO critical for brick and mortar businesses. It used to be called Google Places, and a lot of people refer to this as Google Maps. When a user does a search like Mexican restaurant, St. Charles, Missouri, they're going to see that red bubble pop up on a map with several different Mexican restaurants listed in the area. They can scroll through and they can click on any of those bubbles for more detail.

With the Google My Business (GMB) page, it has key information about the restaurant like hours of operation and phone number, as well as a really nice photo capability so it's a great place for people to share pictures, including from the business. But what's really important about GMB is it's probably the most important user review site on the internet.

When people write a review on GMB they have to have a Google account which they're going to have if they've ever signed up for a Gmail account. Google bought Zagat a few years ago. So a restaurant can request to become Zagat rated through their Google My Business listing.

GMB is very powerful because it ties into the other Google tools that are important for marketing your restaurant, such as Google AdWords. If you are the owner of a verified local Google My Business Page, you can create offers using the new Google post feature.

Instagram and Snapchat are both surging social platforms that warrant consideration. Instagram is a visual sharing app that is now owned by Facebook, so it makes sharing photos and videos using a smartphone extremely easy.

Snapchat is a photo messaging app that allows you to create geo-filters, send on premise snaps, and share coupons and promo codes.

Pinterest is kind of the sleeper of the whole bunch. It's a visual bookmarking site where you build pinboards. You can pin different pictures to different boards. You can organize pins into boards which are simply different categories.

Pinterest is really powerful for restaurants because people love to take pictures of food, they love to talk about great recipes, or events they've attended. Pinterest gives restaurants an opportunity to cover anything from healthy recipes, pictures of their menu items, event ideas, and so forth in a place that's highly shareable.

With any of these social media platforms, restaurants should focus on really tying in to the lifestyle that is important for the people who are using (and sharing) on social media.

People love to talk about social events and post pictures about the events that are important in their lives: weddings, high school reunions, or just a group of friends getting together. Food and restaurants are often a big part of those experiences.

2 SOCIAL MEDIA STRATEGY

Developing a Social Media Strategy

Every successful marketing plan begins with a strategy. Articulating your vision, determining what makes you different from your competitors, and defining your target audience are essential. It's important to determine who your potential customers are, especially if your lunch crowd is different from your dinner crowd, or your catering customers. Who your customers are for different segments of your business impacts how you can use social media for your restaurant.

There are ways you can use social media management tools to simplify the management of social media. But really the best thing is to select one or two social media platforms that are going to work well for your business.

Social media marketing for a restaurant should include a social media plan and a social media policy. The social media plan should include a content schedule, what types of posts to do, and what platforms to use. The policy should address who is authorized to post, reply to comments, and what topics are restricted.

Some things that you post can be scheduled. You also need to plan for posting throughout the day as people are at your restaurant sharing their experiences.

Roles and responsibilities should be assigned depending on your staffing and how comfortable managers are with using social media. Once you have an idea of what your staff is capable of and what you are comfortable having them do as a manager, you can take start to post on multiple social media sites.

Social media sites all have a different purpose and they potentially reach different target audiences. Your goal is to reach your target customers by developing an effective presence on the sites your customers are using.

It's also important to determine what you will post about and what to avoid (like politics or religion), how you will respond to posts and reviews, and the frequency and timeliness of posting and responses.

Does a Restaurant's Potential Target Audience Matter in Terms of the Strategy?

If you're a family restaurant or a restaurant that's located close to a college campus, you probably have different marketing strategies in mind based on different ideal customers. If you're near a college campus you may rely on a large walk-in population. If you're a family oriented restaurant, you may rely on getting customers to come to your restaurant after soccer practice or for other family events.

It's really important to understand who your target customers are, where they're spending time online and developing a strategy to use the right social media sites to reach them. You certainly need to think about the impact of what you post and what you should avoid posting.

You need to take into consideration the type of restaurant you have. You're likely to use social media differently if you are an upscale restaurant. If you are part of a chain you've likely got some additional management issues that you may need to work out as part of a chain in terms of brand standards, management control, and consistency.

Consider where your customers are coming from. Is

your restaurant likely to attract tourists? Will they mostly be locals? If the majority of your customers live locally and already patronize your restaurant, an app like TripAdvisor may not be important to you.

If you're close to a downtown convention center or in an area that has a lot of hotels, you want to make sure you have a strong presence on apps like Yelp and TripAdvisor, as well as a Google My Business listing. You want to be findable when visitors to your town are looking for restaurants. Visitors need to find someplace to eat and they're going to be using Google Maps (Google My Business) or Apple Maps, or they're going to look at an app like Yelp or TripAdvisor.

So knowing whether you want to attract locals, tourists/visitors, or both, will help determine which social media sites you use.

Why Customers Follow Restaurants on Social Media

The number one reason why people follow or like a business on social media is because they're looking for a deal. They want to be able to sign up for a coupon, discount or special offer. Special offers are why people will initially click the like button for the first time or start following a restaurant on Twitter or Instagram.

Other reasons why people might be interested in using social media for restaurants is because people love to share their experiences. The people who have been early adopters of using social media and smartphones tend to be people who share their experiences more on the social networks.

Active social media users rely on the social proof that a restaurant is a good choice and one they recommend.

Posting about the restaurant often serves as a testimonial for the restaurant, even if a customer is just posting a picture of their meal without an actual review.

Likewise, people may posts comments about a restaurant a particular menu item to warn other people about a negative experience.

How do People Use Social Media to Find a Restaurant?

If you're specifically concerned about price, then that's a feature that Google My Business, Facebook and Yelp give users. It's pretty easy to identify what kind of price range you're going to be dealing with that as part of the criteria of what you're looking for.

More and more people are finding restaurants using mobile devices, smartphones or tablets. When people do a search using a mobile device, whether it's with a search engine or whether it's with an app, they're usually making a buying decision within an hour roughly 70% of the time.

That means that if you're a restaurant you definitely need to be taking advantage of some key apps that people use to look for restaurants deals specifically. You also need to take advantage of the apps people use on their phones to search by location like Google Maps, Apple Maps, Yelp and Foursquare.

Users may also do a Google or Siri voice search. There are different searches that people do using voice search, so it is important for restaurants to take advantage of these search opportunities.

If a customer is using a site like Yelp or any other app on their phone, there are pre-built queries that can help them find restaurants that offer that cuisine more quickly.

Yelp has a very strong restaurant search feature built into the app for smartphones. When you go into Yelp, you can make a choice to look for a specific type of category of restaurant or for restaurants nearby.

When people do a search for a specific cuisine, such as Indian or Vietnamese, they are going to use a search engine or an app like Urbanspoon or Yelp.

Why Restaurant Reviews are So Important

Restaurant reviews provide social proof. They are as trusted as a recommendation from a friend or family member. As a Yelp user, when I'm travelling in a different city or neighborhood, I often choose a restaurant based on Yelp reviews. One of the first things I do is open my Yelp app and look for nearby restaurants. Then I scan through the reviews to see what people are saying about a specific restaurant.

Just because I find a restaurant on Yelp doesn't mean that that's the one I go to. There are usually four or five different choices. My decision is usually based on the quality of the reviews and the pictures of menu items that users have posted.

I also use Google to find restaurants and check the different reviews that are posted. Google reviews actually have a big impact in terms of search engine optimization and how well your listing is going to be displayed on Google. Reviews on Google help with search rank based on the overall review rating as well as the number of reviews, currency of reviews (recently posted or posted several months ago), and whether the reviews are replied to by the restaurant.

People can write a review on the Facebook page for a particular restaurant. Those reviews are going to show up more prominently and are often pulled into the Google listing in a Google search.

Twitter is another site where people are having conversations about restaurant experiences. While Twitter posts may be fleeting, having somebody mention your restaurant either positively or negatively on Twitter creates searchable content, especially when users include a hashtag.

On Twitter, any tweet is public because it's posted on Twitter.com. That means every tweet is searchable by anybody and anybody can stumble across a particular tweet. There is a time decay, you're only going to have a few days of tweets you can go back and search through without using some more sophisticated tools.

Because it is pretty easy to find and share tweets, the reach of a tweet can dramatically be increased. As a result, social media monitoring is very important to amplify positive conversation and engagement, or to respond to negative feedback in a timely manner and let people know you care.

How to Make Your Restaurant Interesting on Social Media

As I mentioned earlier, the number one reason people start to follow a business on social media is to claim a deal or offer. So restaurants should definitely start with a special offer.

The timeliness of posts is what helps a restaurant stand out. Posting when people are active on social media increases the likelihood that the post will be seen.

Photos and video are becoming a really important component on social media platforms. Restaurants should post pictures of their daily specials, a video of what is happening in the restaurant, and other visually appealing content.

Photos and videos are really important because they tend to display more prominently in the news feeds and get more engagement which also helps with the reach of the post. You can also have customer testimonials show up as Facebook posts or you can tweet them out. You can interview customers and share those videos on social media.

There are many ways to use social media that are easy to implement. Having a strategy, creating a content calendar, and making assignments of who will post helps restaurants develop a regular social media rhythm.

Let the personality of the restaurant come through when using social media. People are more likely to engage in content that seems authentic and not canned. This is where an independent restaurant might be able to stand out from a chain, unless that chain lets the local store post.

Another key thing to consider is to get user generated content. Give your customers a reason why they should share their experiences on social media and have reminders posted throughout your restaurant. Reminders can be put on tables and on signs above or beside the cash registers. User generated content can increase the reach of a post because it reaches social media users who may not like or follow your restaurant but see the content because it was posted by a friend.

Considerations For Independent Restaurants and Chains

One big consideration for a chain is there is often a managed presence from a corporate office. The local facility may or may not have quite as much control over their social media content as what's being put out by the corporate office. In fact, some chains don't allow local Facebook pages for their individual locations. That's both good and bad.

It's good in the sense that if they're part of a chain they probably have a big enough staff to have a fulltime social media management presence and that's a really nice feature. But at the same time, that social media marketing might not align with what's going on in a local market or a local neighborhood.

A case in point, if the local team is in the World Series, a restaurant should probably be tweeting, "Hey, come in for tonight's special and watch the World Series game on our big screen TV." And of course, the tweet should include the local team hashtag. That's a great way to get people to come into the restaurant and have a social experience about something that's very meaningful to the community. A chain restaurant may or may have enough local awareness to capitalize on that opportunity.

I think in certain respects an independent restaurant may actually have an advantage in terms of what's possible for them on social media. The downside for them is that they don't have the management support that a chain or a multi-location restaurant might be able to provide.

In my opinion, franchises can tie the hands of local

locations if they lock down social media too much, especially when it comes to local search. Facebook, Yelp and Google My Business are so important for reviews – which really help with local search and building trust about the location – that franchises need to balance controlling the brand image while allowing the dynamic aspect of what is happening locally in the store.

Social Media Does Not Replace Other Types of Marketing

Social media has been seen as a silver bullet – stop everything else and all the business has to do is social media. Social media is fantastic but it's not usually enough to make a restaurant thrive or survive.

Social media is certainly important but every restaurant already has variety of marketing items that they print or post like menus, table cards, and cash register receipts.

Integrating social media with the collateral materials that already exist in your restaurant is very important. In fact, it's important for printed materials to make it easy for people to follow your restaurant and to get customers to do social media calls to action, like snap their food, or check-in on Facebook.

If you're still getting traction out of running a coupon in a flyer, newspaper or magazine, I think you can get even more out of it if you integrate social media as a part of that strategy. You can add a social element to any ad that you're running in those types of publications.

Social media is seductive in a sense because it's free and its relatively easy to use. You get a lot of feedback immediately about what's going on, things like likes, comments and retweets. If you're starting your restaurant page on Facebook, you have a pretty good idea of when someone posts or likes your page. And that's a pretty cool feeling.

The metrics that you see on social media are the frequent, tangible results. They're great because you can see that there are things happening but they may not be the right metrics to use to make sure you have long term success.

Again, it's going to come back to your target audience and who your likely customers are. Social media can really help you find your target audience. It can also help you see if you are reaching and engaging your target audience.

3 FACEBOOK

Facebook is the one social media site your restaurant must use. While space in the Facebook newsfeed can be very competitive, a restaurant must use Facebook to posting engaging content and to build a loyal audience. Given that Facebook is the most popular social media platform, it is easy for the posts from your business to get lost in all of the other content on Facebook.

There are Five Things Every Restaurant Owner Should Do Immediately on Facebook:

Number One: Have a really nice cover photo. That's the big photo that sits on top of your page. You can use the cover photo to showcase your menu items or the atmosphere of your restaurant. Also include text over the top of some gorgeous pictures of the interior of your restaurant or of people having fun in a great environment. Facebook also gives you the option to add a video instead of a cover photo.

Number Two: It's really important that your Facebook page is properly set up. For a restaurant, you should set it up as a local business page using the Restaurants & Cafes template. That gives you the ability to display your hours of operation and your address and phone number in a prominent position on your Facebook page.

The Restaurants & Cafes template is designed to highlight your photos and provide your menu, with the Primary Button of Call Now. Additional buttons on the toolbar include: Unlike, Follow, Share, Save.

Facebook allows restaurants to upload a copy of their menu. They limit them to 1 MB so the file (PDF or photo) needs to be fairly small. You can only have one menu loaded at a time so if you have lunch and dinner menus, you will need to consider consolidating those.

Tabs give you a space to feature your photos, business details and more. The default tabs for this template include:

- Home – The main landing area for your Facebook page.
- Photos – Shows photos you've uploaded onto your page.
- Reviews – Shows reviews on your page and allows people to write reviews.
- Offers – Lists current offers for your business.
- Posts – Shows all of your posts, including videos, photos and more.
- Videos – Shows videos you've uploaded onto your page.
- Events – Lists your upcoming events.
- About – Gives people an overview of your page.
- Community – Shows friends' posts and public posts about your Page.
- Jobs – Lists job openings for your business.

Make sure to select the categories that best describe your restaurant.

Number Three: Create at least one custom application on your Facebook page. I recommend creating a couple of different applications. A custom application is something you build with a third party tool that integrates with Facebook. For example, you can have a custom app for a photo contest. Or you can pull in your Pinterest page or YouTube channel into your Facebook page. You can create a custom HTML page on your Facebook page. Or add an email sign-up form so people can join your email list to find out about specials and events. Apps are displayed along the left hand side of your Facebook page.

Number Four: Implement a strategy to make sure that you're posting your daily specials. Do it in time to really peak people's interest. For example, post at 3 o'clock in the afternoon what your dinner special is going to be. People start to get a little tired at work and start thinking ahead to dinner so posting at 3 o'clock is a great way to attract customers to visit your restaurant after work.

Number Five: Take advantage of the posting types, such as sharing photos or videos, creating an offer, doing a live video, creating an event, etc.

Facebook is a fantastic story-telling platform. You can actually build your entire history in a series of timeline posts about your restaurant. It doesn't have to begin the actual day that you opened the door. If you're in a really cool historic building, you could share the history of your restaurant's building.

People will browse your timeline if they're really interested in your restaurant and you should give them a reason to read this. It's a great way to tell your story.

What are the Best Content Ideas for Restaurants to Use on Facebook?

Use Photos and Videos – According to RivalIQ's 2017 Social Media Benchmark report, the most common type of post from a restaurant is photo. Surprisingly, video is seriously under-utilized. Another surprising result of the

RivalIQ study is that Food and Beverage brands post the least on Facebook out of the industries studied.

It's not surprising to find that photos are the most common type of post from the restaurants. Photos get great engagement and seem to get more prominence in the newsfeed.

Pictures are really important on Facebook. If it's a cold rainy day and you have chili at your restaurant, post a picture of your chili. Pictures are everything. Facebook users engage the most when there is a picture posted. Engagement definitely has an impact on the visibility of a post.

Given that video is under-utilized, restaurants that use video on Facebook have an advantage. Video typically outperforms all other post types so posting videos may help your restaurant show more prominently in the newsfeed.

How Can I Make Sure My Facebook Posts are Being Seen?

The best way to make your posts seen by a lot of people is to have an active and engaged group of followers on your Facebook page. Not everybody that likes your page is going to see the posts in their personal Facebook newsfeed, but the likelihood increases if they actively engage with your posts on Facebook – like, comment, and share. When people do engage with your posts reply back to keep the engagement going.

Facebook has become so popular that it can be hard to get posts seen in your customers newsfeed. So it makes sense to consider Facebook advertising, which I cover later in the chapter. Another thing that you can ask the people who like your page to do is to add your restaurant page to their "see first list" so that your posts will always be at the top of their newsfeeds.

To use see first from your News Feed preferences:
1. Click Prioritize who to see first
2. Select a person or Page to see first

To use see first from a profile or Page:
1. If you're not already following the profile or Page, click Follow near their cover photo
2. Hover over Following or Liked near their cover photo
3. Select See First

Note: Users can select up to 30 people or Pages to see first.

When it's appropriate, you can tag people or other pages in your posts. While this can be seriously abused, when done judiciously it can really improve your visibility and reach in the newsfeed. People and pages that are tagged get a notification in Facebook.

It's much more important to have a small but engaged audience than it is to have a large audience that was built by getting people to like your page once, and then never engage again. If someone liked your page but hasn't engaged in any recent posts, the posts from the restaurant page are basically invisible in their newsfeed. So it's really important to post engaging content to increase engagement.

Coupons and Special Offers

Facebook gives you a special type of status update, called an offer. Facebook offers do not cost anything to run so you have control over the terms and the discount.

Facebook offers will be seen by the people who have liked your page. When you use Facebook, you set your own parameters. You decide how long a special offer runs, define your terms and conditions and set your discount. Special offers can also be promoted using paid Facebook Ads.

What Is the Best Way to Advertise on Facebook?

Facebook is really interesting in terms of advertising opportunities because it has such powerful targeting criteria. The reality is that using Facebook for business means that to consistently reach beyond the few truly engaged followers that you have, you need consider paid Facebook Advertising.

One way to create an ad is to "boost" the post. Let's take an offer as an example. When you create an offer, it is only going to be displayed to the people who like your page. If you want to increase the reach of that offer, you can click the Boost Post button after the post has been created. This allows you to use simple criteria for targeting and set your budget and timeframe for the ad.

Boosting a post is a quick way to increase the reach of a post. I think doing a boosted post for a few bucks to promote a special of the day in a small radius or even within a zip code would be worth considering for a restaurant. Facebook makes it simple to do a boosted post right from the post in the newsfeed.

You can create a variety of ads through the Facebook Ad Manager. As a restaurant owner, you can take a post that you created on your Facebook page and turn it into a Facebook Ad, or you can create ads from scratch.

Facebook Advertising Targeting Criteria

In terms of targeting, you can choose geography, different age ranges, or based on gender. The fact is, Facebook has amazing targeting criteria for ads. The following is a high level list, most appropriate for restaurants:

- Location – city, zip code, target by radius from a city, or even choose cities or zip codes to exclude
- Demographics – based on the personal information people have shared in their profiles including age, gender, relationship status, education and the type of work they do
- Interests – pulled from the information people have added to their timelines, the apps they use, keywords from the pages they like, the ads they've clicked, and more.
- Behaviors – these are constructed from someone's activity on Facebook as well as from offline activity provided by third-party providers.

Facebook advertising gets really interesting by using advanced audiences that can be created by:

- uploading a list of your current customers using email addresses or mailing addresses
- building custom audiences from your website visitors (using Facebook's remarketing pixel)
- building lookalike audiences from people who are similar to your customer or prospect list, page fans, or website visitors

With some expertise and analysis of ad performance you can target your ideal customers to maximize your ad spend.

Want to run an ad to only those people who have

visited your website in the last 60 days and are in a specific location? You can with Facebook. You know these people are already interested in your restaurant because they visited your website, so this makes your ad more likely to perform well.

Want more customers like the ones you already have? Use a lookalike audience built from either your existing page likes or your email list. Facebook will build a list of users that are similar to the people you use to base the lookalike on (existing fans or existing email addresses).

Facebook ads are great for any restaurant to consider using. But do them with a purpose. Don't fall into the trap of boosting posts and never creating real ad campaigns. A lot of businesses get frustrated when they spend money on Facebook ads and don't get the results they expect. Using targeting to deliver your ads to the right audience in the right place at the right time will make your ad budget much more effective.

Types of Facebook Ads

Facebook has many different ad types, based on the objectives of the ad campaigns. For more information I recommend you check out the Facebook Ads Guide: https://www.facebook.com/business/ads-guide.

Ad types that work well for restaurants include ads based on photos, videos, and creating a carousel. Note these can be done for both Facebook and Instagram. Page like ads are popular, but keep in mind that page likes don't guarantee that your content will show up in that users news feed if they don't remain engaged with your posts.

A couple of other ad types to consider are Facebook Lead Ads and Facebook Local Awareness Ads.

Facebook Lead Ads

Facebook Lead Ads are designed to be super easy for the person viewing the ad – in fact, completing a call to action can be as simple as two taps. As more people are using Facebook on their phones, Facebook Lead Ads simplify the process of contacting a business to learn more about their products and services.

Facebook Lead Ads work by displaying the ad on Facebook based on the targeting criteria selected. Once someone clicks on the lead ad, a form opens up with the Facebook user's information automatically populated, such as name and email address. The Facebook user can simply press submit if they are happy with the auto-populated information, or they can edit it before they submit. The form is designed to load quickly on a mobile device.

Once the Facebook user submits their form, I recommend creating a trigger to initiate an email with an offer back to the user, via an email marketing platform like Mailchimp. Since the form was automatically populated, the email address that the user submits is likely to be accurate because they initiated the request by clicking on the Facebook Lead Ad to receive an offer. This is a great way to get customers in the door and to build your email list for future email marketing campaigns.

Facebook Local Awareness Ads

These ads are designed to reach people near your business. These ads target your ideal customers using distance, age, gender, and other criteria that you set.

I recommend using the Call Now button, tied to a call tracking number. Additional calls to action include: Like Page, Get Directions, Learn More, Send Message, and Save.

A Facebook Local Awareness ad is displayed on Facebook based on the geographic, age and gender targeting criteria selected. Once someone clicks on the Call Now button, the call is placed to your business.

If you choose to run the ad in the mobile news feed only display option you can also use clicks on the Call Now button to send a text opt-in message to build your text message marketing list. Since the ad only runs in the mobile news feed, you know the call was from a cell phone so you can text them to opt-in to receive text message offers. This gives you an offer to get potential customers in the door faster and it allows you to build your text marketing database.

Facebook Ad Placement

Facebook ads can be delivered in the newsfeed, in the right column, and even on Instagram (if your Instagram account has been integrated with your Facebook Page). You can also choose to run your ads on desktop computers, mobile devices, or both. You can also control the times your ads run.

What Are Whisper Codes and How Do I Use Them to Drive Business?

Whisper codes are just things that you can do as part

of a status update. Let's say it's Wednesday at 11:30 a.m. and nobody is in your restaurant and you're usually really hopping at that time. You can do a post on Facebook like: "Hey, mention this code when you come in and you'll get a free appetizer." Or, "You'll get 10% off your meal today."

Whisper codes are a very informal thing. There's nothing else to do. There are no terms or conditions to offer. Just come in today, mention this code and you'll receive the offer. You can use it as a way to drive people to your restaurant around special events, like to watch a World Series or a football game, or to help increase business during slow periods.

How Does My Target Customer Matter in Terms of Facebook Strategy?

If you're close to a college campus, you're obviously going to have a lot of content that's a bit more informal, casual and fun. If you're an upscale, high end seafood restaurant, you're probably going to convey a more professional and formal tone.

Social media plays an important role in the know, like, and trust stages. Showing off your restaurant using social media and the feedback you get from customers is important for your online image and reputation.

How Can a Restaurant Use Facebook to Drive Catering?

With catering, there are a couple of things to consider. One is, when working with the groups that you are catering for, make sure that you're helping them post content that helps both of you on Facebook.

Second, if a client has created a Facebook event for an event that you're catering, make sure that they include you in their posts about the description of the event and tag your page if possible.

You can tag another Facebook page. When people get together for a social event, they usually are going to be tagging each other in photographs, but you can also tag pages. And you can now use hashtags on Facebook.

It's important for you, as a caterer, to make it as easy as possible for people to know what your Facebook page is and how they can tag your page. That way they can like your page and mention it if they like your food when they're talking about an event and their experience.

How Can a Restaurant Encourage Customers to Check-In, Write a Review, or Post Status Updates

Asking them is the first step. A great way to do that is the signage in your restaurant. Facebook has both check-in and review capabilities. If you're really big on Facebook, I would definitely post signs saying, "Please check-in (or review us) on Facebook."

What that check-in is going to do is provide a status update from the person who's checking in. That check-in is going to be shared with their Facebook friends. Since their friends are probably not following your restaurant on Facebook new potential customers are reached. If I see a friend has checked in to a restaurant on Facebook, it definitely makes me consider visiting that restaurant.

To make check-ins more likely, consider doing a social good program, where whenever someone checks in it counts toward a donation to a cause your restaurant supports. Using signage and the appropriate hashtag is important to help remind people to check in.

I see a lot of missed opportunities for restaurants. There is a tendency, regardless of the social media platform, to do what's called a post and ditch. What happens is that the restaurant does a status update but then nobody monitors it in a timely manner to see if anybody comments on it. So they miss the opportunity to have a discussion, which deepens engagement.

Replying to posts and comments does a couple of things. It builds social proof and it also makes posts more visible because it takes up more physical space on the newsfeed. A string of comments naturally draws people's attention. Since people are already engaging it makes others more likely to engage in that conversation as well.

What Are Some Common Mistakes Restaurants Make Using Facebook?

There are a lot of good reasons to schedule posts. A restaurant can easily develop a regular schedule for posts that revolve around things like daily specials. People who are interested come in for the lunch or dinner special. Having a regular post schedule for posting the lunch special at 9:30 or 10 o'clock in the morning and the dinner special at around 3 o'clock makes a lot of sense.

When you schedule an update then you need to make sure that you're going to monitor the comments and the likes that are happening after the post.

Restaurants need to ask people to like them on Facebook. The Facebook page URL or "Like Us on Facebook" should be prominently displayed on everything they hand to their customers. It should be posted on their menus and receipts. It's not enough to say, "Like us on

Facebook." Tell your customers the exact Facebook URL that they need to go to in order to like your page.

The best time for everybody to have that content created is when the customer is still in the restaurant. Preparing your staff to encourage customers to share their experience can go a long way toward getting more interaction on Facebook.

Facebook Custom Apps

When people go to Facebook, they go there to hang out and spend some time. They don't want to be taken to an external website. So when you're doing anything on Facebook you want to try and keep them inside of Facebook. If you end up directing them to another location, they may go focus on something other than your business.

Apps allow you to have a page that shows your daily specials or to pull in any page from your website. You could have a coupon and a sign up form to receive special offers by email. Photo contests are great and there are apps for that. You could have a user contest where customers upload a photo of their meal and get their friends to vote for it as the most popular picture. This could be run as a contest or sweepstakes. Those are popular applications that you could add to your page.

User Generated Content

The holy grail of marketing for a restaurant is when your happy customers post about their experience: photos, videos, reviews, comments, and check-ins. At that point they are becoming advocates for your business and letting people know that far exceeds the reach of your social media presence.

One great way to get customers talking about your restaurant is to implement a social good program. Ask customers to post about the charity that you are supporting using a hashtag and make sure that they tag your restaurant. Programs like Causley make it easy to implement a social good program simply by having customers check-in and post, which adds up to a full or partial contribution for the cause.

The key to success for any restaurant is to develop a strategy to facilitate the creation of user generated content and build brand advocates. This will help build loyal customers and expand the awareness of your restaurant through know, like and trust.

4 TWITTER

What is Twitter and Why Does it Matter?

Twitter is an online social networking site where users post and interact using "tweets" – 140 character messages. Users can include photos and videos, as well as links to web pages and blog posts. When you tweet that tweet is put into the Twitter feeds of people who follow you. It is all about followers and being followed on Twitter, as opposed to liking and friending on Facebook.

You can follow anybody on Twitter as long as their profile is not private. If you know someone's user name you can follow them, or tweet to them. Twitter makes it very easy to retweet. Retweeting means you share someone else's tweet with your followers.

Every tweet that is posted on Twitter is visible and searchable except for direct (private) messages between Twitter users. You can search every tweet on Twitter even if you're not following a user.

Restaurants should be monitoring for search phrases or hashtags used in tweets, like "What's for dinner?" You can actually tweet back to somebody if you see they have posted "What's for dinner" in their tweet with a suggestion to come in to your restaurant and even offer an incentive to do so.

With Twitter you can set up searches by keyword phrases, you can follow people by their user names, or you can use a hashtag. Hashtags are really just a way to categorize a conversation. Let's take the World Series. If you're a fan of the team in the series, you can follow a hashtag like #STLCardinals or #STLCards. A hashtag is the # symbol followed by a phrase with no spaces. You can either post with that hashtag or you can search by that hashtag to find out what everybody is tweeting who is using that hashtag. Hashtags allow users to follow the twitter conversation around a particular topic.

What You Should Monitor on Twitter

You certainly want to monitor what people are saying if they're mentioning you by your user name, hashtag, or keyword phrase on Twitter. You also want to make sure you monitor based on your restaurant's name, but you can also monitor what people are saying about your competition.

If there are any major local events that are happening you might be able to get people into your restaurant if you are use the hashtag for the event. You can find out what industry influencers are talking in the restaurant industry or get ideas for recipes.

Because anything that somebody says on Twitter is searchable, you can take advantage of an opportunity when you see that someone had a bad experience with a competitor. For example, you could tweet to the twitter user who wasn't happy with a competitor to give your restaurant a try and include a "try us" offer. But you should also address someone's experience with your restaurant.

Twitter Ads

One of the really great features of Twitter's advertising platform is that you can set up tweets that will run as ads. This is an example of a promoted tweets based on what people are tweeting.

Twitter gives an example on their website in regard to

Twitter advertising. If you see somebody tweet, "I just had the worst cup of coffee I've ever had this morning." You set up a Twitter ad to be posted based on that tweet using keyword phrases triggered by that user tweet. Your tweet will automatically be promoted out to that user. Something like, "Hey, we're sorry you had a bad experience, come in and have a cup of coffee on us," or "have a cup of coffee at half price on us today." I don't know of any other advertising platform that gives you the opportunity to take advantage of the sentiment that somebody is expressing as its occurring.

What Type of Restaurant Customer is Twitter Going to Appeal To?

Twitter users tend to be younger and/or tech savvy customers. Younger users tend to use Twitter more than Facebook because they don't want their parents to see what they're posting.

Twitter can be a great channel for targeting professionals, tech savvy people, college students or high school students. Definitely factor in who your target customer is before deciding whether or not to use Twitter.

How to Get the Most From 140 Characters

A hundred and forty characters sounds very limiting but you can upload a picture or video, add a link to a webpage and it will show up in the twitter feed. You can provide a link directly to your website or even a specific page on your website. For example, if you had a coupon on your website that you wanted people to go download and print off, you could tweet that out and have a link taking people right to the page with the coupon.

It's easy to add a link within 140 characters because

you can use a shortened URL. There are several URL shorteners like bit.ly, tiny url, and of course Google and Twitter have their own too.

Using carefully chosen words, you can communicate a great deal in 140 characters. If you get a good review from your local newspaper, you can retweet that or you can tweet a link right to the web page where the review is located – whether it is on the newspaper's website or a Google review. You can also include text in the photo that you upload, which does not fall into the 140 character limitation.

Twitter gives restaurants a way to let people know what's happening in real time. Twitter is a platform that you can use frequently throughout the day and not annoy your followers. If you have a server or somebody who is running the bar who is responsible for helping with social media, they can pretty easily type a 140 character tweet about something interesting that's happening at the restaurant right now.

I strongly encourage restaurants to tweet, especially things like the daily special, events, photos and videos. Video gets the most engagement on Twitter. In general, food and beverage brands do really well on Twitter. So if a restaurant proudly serves a special brand, doing an at mention (@username) of that brand will likely generate a retweet and a like from that brand.

You can post just about anything even when you are limited to 140 characters.

What is the Best Time to Tweet for a Restaurant?

When you use Twitter you can post multiple times throughout the day. Since the average Twitter user's feed gets several tweets a minute, you don't run the risk of Twitter fatigue the way you might with a platform like Facebook.

Tweeting at a specific time of day is going to be tied to what is going on with the restaurant. If you're trying to get people in because you're really slow, just tweet out. You can tweet out a whisper code discount just like you could post it on Facebook.

Using Twitter to Spy on Your Competitors

One way to do this is to create a list of competitors on Twitter. Make sure you set it to be a private list and then you can easily go into the list and see what your competitors are doing. You don't have to follow someone on Twitter to add them to a list. You can also set up a stream to monitor what people are saying about your competitors.

I recommend a tool like Hootsuite for monitoring competitors and to monitor conversations about your business. Hootsuite is a social media management platform which also gives you the ability to manage and post to all of your social media platforms from one single tool. Hootsuite is a great time saver.

Hootsuite allows you to monitor streams of tweets by username, hashtag, keyword phrase, or list. You can do this with Twitter but it's a lot easier to use Hootsuite. You can have a stream that monitors every tweet that mentions the user name of your competitor. You can also include in that stream every mention of the restaurant name spelled out. That way you can see all the things that people are posting on Twitter about a particular competitor.

You can also check for sentiment. If people are

posting things like, "I'm hungry. When are we going to go for lunch?" You can set up a stream to monitor all those conversations and if they're happening close to you, you can tweet to that person. You don't have to be connected in any way to tweet to a particular person. All you have to know is their user name and include it in your tweet. If you know their user name and you include it in your tweets, they're going to see it. They may not notice it because of how many tweets they receive in their Twitter feed, but eventually they will see it because they're going to get a notification when somebody mentions them on Twitter using their user name.

Can You Offer Daily Deals or Special Offers on Twitter?

Absolutely. Twitter was actually one of the most successful social media platforms early on in 2009 when people were first discovering social media. Companies like Dell were very active and tweeting out daily discounts for specific computers or pieces of computer hardware.

Likewise you could easily do the same thing with your restaurant. If you have daily specials tweet those specials daily. You can tweet whisper codes, coupons, etc.

To schedule a tweet on Twitter you can use a solution like Hootsuite. Twitter just added the ability to schedule both organic and promoted-only tweets. If you wanted to schedule Facebook posts in Hootsuite you could do that as well.

5 YELP

Yelp – The User Review Power House

Yelp is a user review based website. I first became aware of it in 2008 here in the Midwest. I'm sure it was happening out on the coasts well before that. The first thing that I saw people really using Yelp for was to share their experiences at restaurants.

Yelp gives people a very easy way to write a review about their experience with a restaurant, post pictures and make recommendations.

As a restaurant owner you can claim your Yelp listing and ensure that your business information is correct on your Yelp listing. Make sure that your address, phone number, and hours are correct. Add the categories that best fit your restaurant. You can post pictures of things that you want to highlight about your restaurant. Claiming your Yelp listing helps you have control over your listing.

You don't have control over what users are writing and that's the beauty of Yelp. Yelp has had some criticism because there were some instances where they found that some reviews weren't necessarily authentic, but Yelp works hard to police reviews.

For the most part, Yelp has been an authentic user driven site and because of that people recognize it is not marketing and advertising. Authentic user reviews appeal to people. People are more likely to believe a write-up about an experience and the menu items they would recommend from somebody that they don't even know rather than paid advertising.

Yelp is important because people rely on reviews to

make decisions, even from strangers. They also get a feel for a restaurant based on the responses the restaurant provides to reviews, both positive and negative. If you're looking to improve your local search engine optimization then Yelp is an important site because it frequently ranks at the top of the first page for many local searches.

Are Customer Reviews Still Important?

Reviews are more important than ever. Customer reviews are extremely important because they have a real impact on people's buying behavior. For example, if you are looking for a Vietnamese restaurant on Yelp and the first four reviews you see are lukewarm at best, you're probably not going to that restaurant.

People will trust reviews even though they don't personally know the reviewers on Yelp. Social media creates a sense of community and a sense of internal policing which tends to keep reviews honest.

Most people tend to use Yelp as an app on their Smartphone. That's the way I typically use it. I use it to help me search specifically for restaurants in areas I'm traveling to or where I'm already at.

You can also use Yelp if you have a desktop computer or laptop. Given that Yelp ranks so well for search, there are many people who click on the Yelp link that is returned on a desktop/laptop for a local search like Mexican restaurant near me. TripAdvisor results can rank really well for these types of searches too.

Yelp allows the user to search for a specific type of business, like restaurants. For restaurant searches, you can choose by a category of restaurant. Results are determined based on the GPS on a cell phone or based on the IP address of the computer user for restaurants that match that category that are nearby.

Be Proactive on Yelp

Beyond claiming your business listing and taking control over the information about your business, it's important to make sure that information is always up to date and accurate, especially hours of operation. Restaurants should continue to upload photos and videos and include a current menu.

Restaurants can also use Yelp to offer deals and sell gift certificates. You can run a deal on Yelp if you pay. It's less expensive to run a deal on Yelp than on Groupon or Living Social. One advantage that Living Social or Groupon has is that they are very active in promoting the deals that are run their platforms through email marketing, and anybody who subscribes to Living Social or to Groupon get an emails with all of the specials that are available in that particular market. You can also search their websites for offers.

With a Facebook offer or Yelp deals, you don't have that extra level of promotion. You will need to promote it or have people find that opportunity because they are Yelp or Facebook users. You can use social media posts, or you can run Facebook or Yelp ads to promote your offers.

Yelp reviews are pulled into the search results when someone is using Yahoo or Bing for their search. Since more than 20% of searches are done using Bing or Yahoo, the Yelp reviews will be the most prominent set of reviews that a searcher will see. Top lists from Yelp also rank very well on Google. So having an effective strategy to get quality Yelp reviews is very important.

6 GOOGLE

Google My Business (GMB) is the most important business listing site on the web for local searches. By claiming and optimizing your business on GMB, you can make sure the information about your business is accurate. You can also add photos and videos to highlight your restaurant.

A quality GMB page will definitely give your restaurant a chance to show up on Google Map results. Getting your restaurant to show up in the three pack (the 3 results that show on Google Maps) when someone does a local search like "BBQ near me" is really important.

There are several things that restaurants can do to make their GMB page stand out. Adding photos and videos of your restaurant is important. You can add interior, exterior, at work, team, branding, and 360 photos. It is important to continue to add new content and make sure your business information is accurate and up to date at all times.

Google 360 photos can be from the street (Google Street View – make sure it is correct) and you can also create 360 videos to provide a virtual tour of the interior of your restaurant. Google 360 video tours of the inside of your restaurant are a great way to build trust in your business by allowing users to experience what your restaurant is like before they visit. If your restaurant has a video tour and your competitors don't, this definitely helps differentiate your business for both potential customers and with Google.

When searching for a business nearly half of users use a mapping product like Google Maps. This shows clear intent to visit a business that the user found on the map.

When there are quality photos and a virtual tour, it is twice as likely to generate interest in that business.

GMB pages recently added the ability to do posts from your GMB page. These posts are different than Google+. The Google Post can include an image, up to 300 words of text, and a call to action button. Posts can be for events (which allows you to include start and end dates and times).

Google Posts can have one of the following calls to action: Learn More, Reserve, Sign Up, Buy, and Get Offer. The call to action includes a link to the appropriate web page.

Using Google Posts, your restaurant could share daily specials or a current promotion, promote an event at the restaurant, highlight news about your restaurant, or give customers a one-click way to make a reservation, sign up for a newsletter, or even buy a product from your website.

Google Posts automatically expire in 7 days or less, or when the event ends. Businesses that are using Google Posts will receive a notification on the 6th day that their post is about to expire.

While Google Posts are a new feature, I believe that restaurants should be using these immediately. Google likes it when businesses use the tools Google provides and Google is the most important business listing site on the web. Google Posts are a likely way to improve your business ranking on Google.

Google+ is another important player in social media marketing. While it is a channel that is often neglected or overlooked, because it is Google, I recommend developing a posting strategy for Google+. It is beneficial to post photos, videos, and links to your website on your Google+ page.

The Importance of Google Reviews

Google reviews are extremely helpful. For restaurants, I believe that Google and Yelp are the two places you must have people writing reviews about your restaurant.

Claiming your GMB and having it show up on the Google map is important for a restaurant because that's where customers are likely to write reviews. From that perspective, having customer reviews show up on Google maps is incredibly important. If you get a lot of people writing reviews about your business on Google, your website and your listing on Google become much more visible.

Google requires the user to sign in before they can write a review. Old reviews that people wrote before Google required sign-ins will list reviewers as a Googler but it won't actually display the actual person. When a user is logged into their Google account and they write a Google review, their name and profile picture will be included.

Remember the concept of social proof. When somebody is reading reviews about a restaurant it influences their decision making. When they know people that have left reviews about a particular restaurant, those reviews on Google are going to sway their opinion even more.

Do Google Reviews have more credibility than the other review sites? That's hard to say. What is certain is that Google is the most important website for people searching for local restaurants. Having a consistent stream of strong Google reviews acknowledged by the restaurant has a very big impact in search results as well as social proof.

I would make it as easy as possible for people to write Google reviews about your restaurant. Create a review funnel as I discussed in the review section. You don't want to make people work hard to find where they can write a review.

I recommend that a restaurant encourage reviews for each individual experience that somebody has. Asking somebody one time when they come in to write a review on Google, the next time to write a review on Facebook, the next time to write a review on Yelp is a good strategy. As long as they're writing about different experiences, I think that is a solid strategy.

Advertising on Google

With Google you always have the option of using Google AdWords campaigns which can be search-based ads or display-based ads. When somebody types in a phrase like 'Mexican restaurant' with a location, you can have your ad show up in the search results. But since you can do an offer through Google Posts you don't necessarily have to pay to advertise.

You can advertise to ensure that when a user does a local search for your type of restaurant, your ad shows up at the top of the search results page. If you do not currently show up on Google Maps or key websites like Yelp or TripAdvisor, or your restaurant does not show up on page one of Google, then using Google AdWords is something to consider.

Google is integrating all of their online properties. If you run an ad on Google AdWords, it's going to tie in with your GMB page to give you additional value and make strong integration between being listed on both of those Google properties.

If you're using a Google AdWords campaign, then you can run that ad based on geographic targeting as well as how much you're willing to pay for a particular set of keyword phrases.

One thing that businesses need to check is to see if they have multiple listings on Google for the same location. Unfortunately this is very common. It is very important to claim and remove or merge the incorrect, old, or partial Google listings to strengthen your GMB page ranking. Many businesses think more listings on Google is better, but it can actually hurt how your business is ranked.

It is very likely that there are multiple listings for a business location on Google but also for other directory sites. Cleaning this up is a real pain and can take several hours. I recommend that a business do a listing audit to find incorrect or duplicate listings and remove them. The best way to find and remove duplicate Google listings is to hire someone who knows what they are doing, or to subscribe to a management tool that will make this process easier.

7 REVIEWS

What Makes Somebody Write a Review?

For Yelp, first they need to be a Yelp user. So restaurants need to make sure that people can get the Yelp app and let people know the restaurant is on Yelp. Google also requires customers to log in to leave a review. People who have written reviews before are more likely to write new reviews.

The customer's experience is usually the catalyst that prompts them to write a review. People tend to write about the extremes they experience, either things that are good or things that weren't good at all, or even very average. The trigger to write the review could be the quality of the food, the quality of the service, the ambiance of the restaurant, or all of the above. Some people write a review just because they like to use the technology and they often do it while they're eating.

If you just let reviews happen, they are going to skew to the negative. People are just more inclined to write a review when we have a bad experience and we tend to take the good experiences for granted.

That's why it's really important to create a review funnel. You need to make it as easy as possible to ask someone to write a review. I recommend setting up a review funnel that drives happy customers to the review sites you want people to write reviews on.

The sites I recommend are Google and Yelp. I would consider adding TripAdvisor and Facebook too. Having a page on your website that includes your review funnel can direct people to the review sites that you choose. This eliminates the hassle of customers having to search for the review sites.

Other restaurant related review sites to consider including in your review funnel are: Fodor's, MenuPages, OpenTable, Restaurant.com, Zagat, and Zomato. If the review sites you want customers to use have apps, make it easy for people to download the app, and even explain to your customers why it might help them with other businesses.

Ask customers to write reviews and make it as easy as possible for them. Many satisfied customers are happy to write a review if you ask them, so make it a habit, and add signage. Print the review link on your menus, table cards, receipts, etc.

Put signs in your restaurant encouraging people to find you and write a review about their experience on Yelp, Google, etc. Yelp users can find the restaurant by using the check-in or clicking the Nearby icon in the Yelp app. Honestly, there's plenty of time when people are sitting at a restaurant for them to write a short review and post a photo with the review.

Some people will write a review even if you don't ask them. They may not always share their dissatisfaction or frustrations with you. That's why having a review funnel is important. It give people a place to provide feedback before they post a bad review. If you use it as a customer service opportunity, you can often turn a negative situation into a positive one, preserving your reputation and retaining a customer.

Remember that having no reviews also speaks volumes about a restaurant. If a restaurant has no reviews, someone who uses reviews to decide what restaurants to eat at will probably not pick one with no reviews.

Restaurants are one of the most reviewed industries, so even a restaurant with few reviews implies that the restaurant must be below average... whether it is or not.

Another really important aspect of reviews and reputation is to monitor what people say about your restaurant. Conversations happen on social media, so setting up Hootsuite to monitor social media is important. But so is monitoring reviews about your business.

Set up a review monitoring system that emails key people whenever a new review is written. Responding to reviews helps make the reviews more legitimate, both with users and with the search engines because it shows you are paying attention. Having a plan on how to handle negative reviews is key. If it looks like responding to a negative review is going to be contentious, respond to take if off line to resolve the customer's issue.

Get customers to write reviews on more than one site. If they write a review on Yelp, they are probably willing to write a review of your restaurant on another review site. Part of it is just an awareness of your staff to prompt people to write a review on a different site.

The most important thing to do is to have a process of asking for and collecting reviews. If you just let reviews happen, they tend to skew to the negative as most people are much more likely to write a negative review because of a bad experience. Unless you get in the habit of asking people for reviews, positive reviews will probably be under-represented.

A Dissatisfied Customer Can Really Hurt Your Restaurant

Reviews are tricky. Studies show that if younger users

see all five star reviews, they are less likely to believe all of those are authentic. Everybody has bad experiences. If you have 30 reviews and all 30 are five star, statistically that's just not very likely to happen.

When potential customers see a review from someone who had a less than stellar experience, if it's not scathing, that negative or lukewarm review doesn't necessarily hurt you if you have several other really strong reviews on the site. As a matter of fact, it may make it look like those other high quality reviews are maybe even a little bit more believable.

If you don't respond to negative reviews, people think you don't care about your customers. You run the risk of backlash when people see that you didn't respond. That review sits there and it festers and it may even make people angry to the point where they decide that they're going to share their negative reviews as well.

But if you take control of a negative review and admit there were some issues that need to be resolved and respond to the user's review saying something like, "We're really sorry you had a bad experience. We want to make it right, so next time you come in we'll give you 50 percent off your meal," you're trying to make a less than stellar situation right. People really respect that and they typically respond positively.

You may occasionally find situations where somebody just has an axe to grind. Maybe they had a really bad day and the more you try to resolve their problem, the angrier they become. That's a risk you run but I think it's much better to respond to a review than to ignore it. When you are proactive and focus on making a bad experience right, you have the opportunity to retain customers rather than drive them away by ignoring them.

Accuracy of Business Listings

An important factor in the reputation of a restaurant is the accuracy of the information about the business on directory listing sites across the web. These sites send strong signals to search engines that your business information is accurate, consistent, and up to date. There is so much inaccurate data about businesses posted online, it is essential that the data about your business, especially key elements like Name, Address, and Phone (called NAP), along with business hours can be a real difference maker.

With so many people using GPS and navigation apps to find businesses, you need to make sure your location on navigation apps is also accurate. The pin on the map for your location needs to be correct to make sure customers can easily find you.

Maintaining your menu online can also be a challenge too. I strongly recommend one of the many directory management tools to manage all of the information about your business. That way you publish once and accurate and up to date information is pushed to dozens of key directory listing sites, including Facebook, Yelp, Yahoo, Google My Business, and Foursquare. The information you can publish includes menus, photos and videos, updated hours and holiday hours, and even featured messages and specials.

8 INSTAGRAM

Any chapter on Instagram has to start with the power of visual marketing. 65% of humans are visual learners. Visual marketing is now one of the foundational elements of any marketing strategy. People remember images more than things they hear and most humans are visual learners. Hubspot provides some amazing statistics on visual marketing content in one of their blog posts - https://blog.hubspot.com/marketing/visual-content-marketing-strategy.

It's no surprise that Instagram has become one of the most popular social media platforms and typically has the highest engagement rates. Instagram provides an easy way to capture, edit and share photos, videos and messages.

Instagram has become one of the most popular social media platforms with younger audiences, who might use Facebook sparingly. So it is important for restaurants to consider how to use Instagram based on target customers.

Using Instagram to market a restaurant makes a lot of sense. People love to share pictures of food. Food is social. Instagram has considerably higher engagement rates in the Food & Beverage industry according to a 2017 Social Media Benchmark report by RivalIQ.

There are several ways that a restaurant can use Instagram. Using hashtags is very important when posting on Instagram. In fact, Instagram is a platform where it is acceptable to use several hashtags in your post. Some ideas for hashtags for restaurants to use include:

- #todayspecial
- #lunchspecial
- #hangry
- #friyay
- #yum
- #giveaway

- #eatright
- #[restaurant name]
- #[special food item]
- #[special drink item]
- #food
- #foodporn
- #foodie
- #delish
- #thatawkwardmoment
- #dessert
- #chocolate
- #ValentinesDay
- #[day of the week]
- #yummy
- #foodgasm
- #nom
- #[type or restaurant]
- #treatyoself

The quality of the images and videos you post matter, so it is important to take the time to compose these. Presentation matters, so consider the rule of thirds, lighting, contrast, etc. when taking pictures. Instagram gives you filters and photo-editing that can be used as appropriate.

I recommend that restaurants post pictures and videos to highlight menu items, specials, coupons, dining room ambiance, staff members, and what's happening in the restaurant. Write captions to tell a story, ask for feedback, ask questions, use emojis, or explain the photo.

You can share Instagram posts to Twitter and Facebook, so be mindful that comments over 140 characters will be cut off when posted on Twitter. Other Instagram sharing options include email, Tumblr, Flickr, and Foursquare.

With Instagram, I think restaurants have a great opportunity to ask customers to post and share photos and videos taken at the restaurant. Let customers know what your Instagram user name is so they can tag your restaurant in their post and/or use a branded hashtag.

Get user generated content. Motivate customers to

post on Instagram by doing a contest, or rewarding great photos with discounts or free items. Get creative and ask your customers to be artistic or funny, post during live events — anything that helps to show the atmosphere of your restaurant. When users post, make sure you respond.

Give an incentive for Instagram users with larger followings by rewarding customer shares by offering them something. Have those users post a photo that mentions your restaurant (hashtag, username, even a Foursquare check-in).

Regram posts! Regramming is the practice of posting a photo from someone else's Instagram account to your own, along with appropriate credit. If a restaurant regrams a photo taken by a customer, it shows that the restaurant is paying attention and it is likely to spur additional user generated content.

A restaurant can also post photos of products they serve from their suppliers and tag those suppliers. For example, if you serve a locally know cheesecake tag the baker. They should see that they were tagged and it will likely prompt some level of engagement from them, such as a like or a comment. They might even regram it!

Instagram contests are great ways to generate activity and engagement. Contests can be simple — like a post to be entered to win — or they can be a little more complex.

A regram contest gives you the opportunity to have users regram a photo of the restaurant's choice, along with tagging the business or branded account. This is a great way to increase your reach to the followers of your followers.

Another easy contest is to do a comment contest,

such as asking for comments like: "tag 5 friends" or "tell us what you'll order if you win."

Instagram advertising is done through the Facebook Ad manager, so all of the great targeting options available on Facebook are also available for Instagram ads. This can provide a very cost effective way to reach new customers or re-engage current customers.

9 SNAPCHAT

What is Snapchat?

Snapchat is a camera app for mobile devices used by 166 million active Snapchatters globally. Pictures, drawings, and videos are called snaps. Users message snaps to their friends to show them what they are up to and how they are feeling – up to 3+ billion snaps every day. Most snapchatters message their close friends every day.

Snaps can be between 1-10 seconds long and then are deleted. According to Snapchat, the average snapchatter spends a total of 25-30 minutes per day, averaging 18 sessions a day. The biggest growth in Snapchat is with users 25 and older. But Snapchat is most commonly used by teenagers and young adults into their thirty's.

How to use Snapchat for a Restaurant

For a restaurant, Snapchat is a great platform to let the world know about your business on mobile. In fact, about 80% of snapchatters say they use Snapchat in restaurants. Since there is such strong engagement among close friends Snapchat ads are recommendations.

Other places where Snapchat is used heavily usedinclude:

- 81% at home
- 70% at concerts
- 50% at the gym
- 49% at the airport

Create your Snapchat account with your restaurant's name as the username (you might need to add a city name or neighborhood at the end of the name if the username you want is already taken). Download your Snapcode (a image that users can scan on their phones to follow your restaurant on Snapchat).

Make it easy for your customers to follow your restaurant on Snapchat. Place you Snapcode and username on your restaurant website, menus, flyers, table tops, by the cash register, in the restrooms, add it to email signatures, and on your other social media sites. Have customers scan the code in front of a staff member to receive a bonus or discount.

Snapchat Geofilters

One great way restaurants can use Snapchat is to create a Snapchat geofilter. Snapchat allows a business to create filters specific to your restaurant's geographic location. You can add special logos that will appear over the snapchatter's photo or video, which allows them to add the filter when they send the snap. Filters need to be 1080 by 1920 pixels saved as a .png file.

Benefits of having a Snapchat filter include having your customers advertise your restaurant for you by using the filter for their followers to see. Restaurants can set a geofilter for a specific day to promote a special or deal. This is a really cheap way to advertise your business, where snapchatters are encouraged to snap their experience, including snapping coupons or discounts.

You can also create personal geofilters for special events like weddings, birthdays, or graduations. The average filter costs about $5 per 20,000 square feet.

Make sure to snap your food and beverages, snap the inside of your restaurant, and snap things that are relevant (related to temperature, sporting or cultural events, etc.). You should also encourage your customers to snap as these come across to their friends as recommendations.

Snapchat also has stories that expire after 24 hours. Your restaurant can use stories to create limited time offers by posting coupons that are only valid while your story is live. This creates urgency to come into the restaurant before they expire.

The key to Snapchat is to recognize that it is a fun, playful, and creative platform — so use it that way! Consider gamifying snaps by hiding secret deals in the snaps. Have friends share a snap of their meal with a discount code and hashtag that snapchatter and their friend can both receive the discount.

10 PINTEREST

Pinterest is a visual bookmarking site used to create visual pin boards. It's a way to create a collection of pictures. There are collections or categories and you can create your own boards. You pin pictures to these boards, and you can re-pin pictures from somebody else's board onto your board. It's a highly visual site. Pinterest skews pretty heavily towards female users.

Pinterest is the sleeper in regard to social media. Where Pinterest is really powerful for restaurants is that people love to take pictures of food and they love to talk about great recipes that they've discovered. Pinterest gives a restaurant an opportunity to cover anything from healthy recipes, pictures of their menu items, event ideas, lifestyle ideas, and meals for special events like weddings and class reunions, in a place that's highly shareable.

Pinterest is growing in popularity with men. More and more men are finding it useful to organize pictures. I know a couple of men that are using Pinterest for hydroponics. They're interested in being able to do gardening without having access to a lot of water and using the hydroponic facilities. Pinterest actually has some of the best information you can find out there for hydroponics and so they've become active Pinterest users.

Pinterest is a great opportunity for restaurants because people love to take pictures of their food. They love to see pictures of food. They love to share recipes. Sharing recipes is a very popular on Pinterest. You can post some of your own recipes if you're willing to do that. If not, you can monitor to see what recipes other people are posting to give you ideas for new menu items. If you've got a healthy menu line you can take pictures and you can build a pin board of your healthy menu.

Pinterest is really used heavily for weddings, class reunions, travel planning and other social activities, all of which create an opportunity for restaurants. If you want to get more people to have their wedding reception or other social events at your restaurant Pinterest is a really good way to let them know that you have a facility that might work for their event or group.

On Pinterest, it's really just setting up your pins and asking people to do a certain set of steps in terms of re-pinning. You can run a contest on Pinterest and it's free to do so. It's a little bit more flexible than other sites. They certainly have guidelines that they recommend that you follow but it's not as rigorous as it would be to run a contest on Facebook for example.

Another great way to use Pinterest is for meal planning. So a restaurant could put together some kind of a meal planning check list and on there you could say: "Make sure you eat out once a week at our restaurant."

I think the opportunity for a restaurant to post pictures of all of their menu items and encourage their customers to post pictures of their food and experiences on Pinterest is a great way to build awareness about the restaurant. Pinterest is one of the strongest referring sources of traffic to a website typically, depending on how the pins are set up.

It's also very easy to organize your pin boards on Pinterest and then you can create a custom app on Facebook that will pull in your Pinterest page right onto your Facebook page to where people can look at your Pinterest page without even leaving Facebook. On Facebook you can pull in a YouTube channel and a Twitter feed very, very easily. There are free applications that will allow you to do that.

11 FOURSQUARE

What is Foursquare?

Foursquare is a location-based social networking website that has 2 apps people can use on their phones – Foursquare Swarm and Foursquare City Guides. Users "check in" at venues using Foursquare Swarm by selecting from a list of venues the application locates nearby. Swamp is considered to be a lifelogging app that keeps track of places the user has checked into and offers the ability to collect stickers.

Users can get more information about the restaurant if they want by using Foursquare City Guides, which provides tips about the business, location information, and specials. Photos posted via Foursquare Swarm are included in the Foursquare City Guide listing.

When a user checks-in to a location, the Swarm app let's their friends know that the user has been to that business.

Why is Foursquare Important for Restaurants?

Restaurant should claim their Foursquare listing since Foursquare is still a very important directory listing site that ranks well in search results. Restaurants can add photos and make sure business information including business name, address, phone, industry, and hours of operation are correct. Your restaurant might already be on Foursquare, so claiming the listing and making sure the business information is correct is vital.

Foursquare allows restaurants to create specials that

Foursquare City Guide users can find and claim. The restaurant does not have to pay Foursquare to be able to do this, though it can also run paid ads on Foursquare. Customers can redeem a reward by showing it on their phone.

A check-in is a testimonial – anybody who knows you sees that you have checked in at a restaurant is more likely to go there as well.

Foursquare also gives restaurants a way to give users tips. Tips might include restaurant specialties, special events, and daily specials.

Are Specials on a Foursquare Different Than Groupon or Living Social?

The biggest difference is the fact that you don't have to pay Foursquare to set up a special. If you want to create a special where you're going to give somebody a free appetizer if they buy at least $15 worth of food when they check in, then you're setting the terms of that deal and you're determining what you want to do in terms of a discount.

With Groupon or Living Social you typically have to do a deep discount on your products or services and then split the remaining amount with Groupon or Living Social. The end result might be that you are only collecting around 25% of your original price. That's not good for business and it's not sustainable. The question is still out about whether Groupon or Living Social builds loyal customers for the businesses who use their services.

Deals that are too good can overwhelm a business. There have been restaurants that have been run out of business because too many people redeemed deeply discounted deals and it created major cash flow problems. Foursquare gives you a lot more control over what you choose to offer in terms of a discount. As a result, Foursquare can help to generate return customers.

Foursquare Success Stories

I've worked with a couple of different restaurants that have had Foursquare specials and people love them. People love deals – remember it is the number one reason people follow a business on most social media platforms. Restaurant owners have told me that customers say they visited their restaurant because of a Foursquare special. It was the thing that got them in the door as opposed to going someplace else.

It's very easy to set up a special on Foursquare and very few restaurants do it. That really is a surprise to me because of how simple it is to do. Most restaurants rely on repeat customers. Offering a Foursquare deal can attract both new and repeat patrons. If you're a restaurant it's always easier to get people who already know your business to come back to your business.

While Foursquare may not be as popular as it once was, it is an important site to make sure your business is on. Claiming the Foursquare listing for your restaurant is important because Foursquare listings still rank well for local searches.

12 OTHER SOCIAL MEDIA OPPORTUNITIES

How Can You Integrate Social Media Marketing with Traditional Marketing?

There are many ways to integrate social media with traditional marketing techniques..

Restaurants have a lot of printed marketing materials that you can use to make it easy and convenient for people to find and connect with you on social media. If you have a menu, make sure you have your Facebook URL for your Facebook business page on that menu. If you have printed napkins, make sure you have your Facebook page or your Twitter user name listed right there.

If you have hold music tell people your main social media URL, don't just say like us on Facebook. Don't make people work to find you! I called a pizza restaurant recently and they had hold music. During that hold music they were telling me about the different specials that they had, but they could have also told me what their website or Facebook URL was, but they didn't. They could have asked me do something like, "Go to our Facebook page and click on coupon application for $5 off your order today." That's how you tie social media into the other marketing that you're already doing and too many restaurants aren't taking advantage of this opportunity.

There are a few success stories of restaurants I know in my area. We've got a restaurant here in Saint Charles where I live that I've worked with and they've done a fantastic job of building a Facebook fan base and a Twitter following. Every year during March Madness, there's the St. Charles Patch, a local online news website and they run a contest for the best restaurant in the Saint Charles or the Saint Louis area.

Every year the St. Charles Patch runs a competition just like the final four in college basketball. In this competition restaurants go head to head, and based on the number of people voting for you and sharing their votes on social media, it's is going to determine if you advance to the next round.

The restaurant I worked with won several years in a row because they are very active in using social media to get the word out and they engage their followers. They have an active group of followers that they can tap into and get them engaged. Because of that they've got something really nice to brag about on a billboard that lends a lot of credibility to their restaurant.

One of the main goals of marketing is to stay top of mind so when somebody is ready to make a decision they're already going to be thinking about your business. Social media is one of the best ways to get content out there to stay top of mind.

You can do a lot to build your Facebook fan base by using direct mail. You can incorporate a strategy where whenever you send a direct mail piece with a coupon you ask people to visit your website with even more offers or ask them to like the Facebook page. Don't send the coupon without asking people to do something online.

If you get people on your website (direct mail can be a great way to do this and the website can give you a great way to measure your direct mail effectiveness) you can make it easy for people to like your Facebook page or follow you on other social media sites. You can also use these website visitors to create a website custom audience to use for a cheap send touch ad on Facebook.

You've got a multi-touch strategy. Facebook ads are typically about one-tenth of the cost of direct mail. You should consider both direct mail and Facebook as a touch. That's valuable to the business because now they've got somebody liking their page on Facebook and maybe they joined the email marketing list. In this case, that traffic was all driven because you were using a direct mail piece.

There are a lot of things that people still do in traditional advertising. The best way to have accountability is to drive anything online. Everything online is measurable. With direct mail, the only way to know it is working is if a customer tells you or if they bring in the coupon that was mailed to them. But you really have no idea how many people looked at it and did anything with it other than the people who are redeeming a coupon. Social media gives you better metrics and analytics to be able to determine if what you're doing is working well for you. Using a call tracking system on your website is another great way to measure offline campaigns.

The thing I love about anything online is that if you set it up properly you can measure everything online. This allows you to look at how much you're spending and determine what kind of a return you're getting on that investment. It can provide a way to measure offline campaigns when social media, call tracking, and website analytics are integrated as a part of traditional marketing campaigns.

The other thing that's really powerful about social media, Facebook in particular, is that they can be fantastic tools to build your email marketing list. There have been some recent studies done that show that social media is great in terms of branding and staying top of mind but it hasn't translated into driving a lot of sales.

The Importance of Engagement

Restaurants are in a unique position because buying lunch or dinner is a shorter and much less complicated decision than buying a car for example. Putting a coupon or posting a gorgeous photo of your lunch special on social media is likely to get someone to take immediate action.

If you're going to ask somebody to follow you on social media you've got to give them a reason to want to follow you. So just asking them to follow you is not enough. They actually have to be engaged and interacting with you to really make it a win/win for both of you. Posting relevant and interesting content increases engagement.

Engagement is the critical thing which you need to try to accomplish on social media. By engagement I mean somebody retweeting your tweet or somebody clicking that reaction button on your Facebook post, or better yet sharing it with their friends or writing a comment about it. When you're getting people to interact with your content and engage with you online, your business becomes much more visible.

When it comes to social media, RivalIQ talks about the 3 A's: Audience, Applause, and Amplification. Audience is the collection of people who follow you on social media. It's an important factor to be sure, but having a large audience isn't enough. That's where Applause and Amplification come into play.

Applause is when you get likes on posts on Facebook, Twitter, Instagram, etc. They are helpful in that they provide social proof, but they don't necessarily expand the reach of your posts beyond your current audience.

Amplification happens when people do more than just like posts. They share and comment on them. When people share and comment, they are making that content more interesting and engaging, and they are sharing it with other social media users who might not even know you exist. This has an immediate impact on the reach of your post.

When social media sites see commenting and sharing, it indicates that there must be something useful or interesting about the post, which can also have an impact on the visibility of the post both to your current audience and also through trending topics. On Facebook, a post that has comments takes up more room in the newsfeed which increases visibility.

When people share the posts of the restaurant, or comment on the posts, it dramatically improves the reach of the posts. When users engage, amplification happens and customers and followers can become advocates!

Using Social Media to Create Loyalty Programs

Social media is a great way to build a loyal group of followers. Using social media to create a loyalty program is a logical extension. You can launch a formal loyalty program to nurture customers and increase sales. You can also accomplish some of this based on how you use social media.

Some ways you can use social media to create a loyalty program include:
- Create custom audiences from visitors to your website and use Facebook retargeting to deliver ads with offers only to users who visited your website.

- Use a third party app on Facebook to reward Facebook engagement. This is a great way to increase engagement and to reward active social media users.
- Use Facebook ads with offers delivered only to the people who have liked your page or have joined your email list.

Emerging Technology to Pay Attention to: Chatbots

Chatbots are one of the hottest trends in marketing automation. Here are some reasons to consider the use of chatbots for restaurants:

- More people are on messaging apps than all social apps combined.
- Ability to connect 24/7 with your customers where they are without additional staffing
- Custom promotions (highly segmented)
- Convenient menu
- Conversational reservations
- Feedback
- For the content most requested, the user interface is preferred over stand-alone apps
- Collect email addresses (typically not as easy for a restaurant unless they have a loyalty program)

Here are a few examples of how your restaurant could use chatbots:

Convenient Menu: Since you can have a "menu" of options at the bottom of the chat, you can include a link to your menu. That can either be a pdf, a link to your website menu, or even build the menu in an interactive way into the bot (complete with choices and pics).

Conversational Reservations: These can be like "talking" to a person on the phone. The user provides how many people and what time they would like the reservation. The chatbot provides interactive responses to collect the information needed to make the reservation without anyone at the restaurant having to be involved.

Custom Promotions: Your restaurant could send out an offer or coupon via a bot broadcast to existing members or by using a Facebook ad that makes them click into the bot (which happens to also sign them up). The user then gets the coupon code, or secret word, or picture to show the wait staff to get the offer or coupon.

Restaurants should have promotional materials in the restaurant that prompt customers to message the bot to get the wifi code or to leave feedback on their server or to compliment the chef. Since these bots automate certain activities, they can be real time savers. While they are relatively new, it is a technology that is receiving a lot of attention by the social media platforms.

13 PUTTING THE *SOCIAL* BACK IN SOCIAL MEDIA FOR RESTAURANTS

By: Nina Radetich

When social media emerged (think back to the early days of Facebook), it was designed as a means to keep in touch with friends and family, a digital connector. Never before had we been able to share bits and pieces of our lives with so many people in an instant. Remember those days when we had to print out pictures of the kids and *mail* them to Grandma & Grandpa? Not anymore.

As social media grew in adoption and popularity, it evolved… a lot less connection… a lot MORE broadcasting. I blame brands. When companies discovered social media, many forgot what the word "social" meant. Look at us! Here's what makes us great! Come eat at our restaurant! Many brands saw social media as simply another advertising opportunity.

It's easy to broadcast. It's not as easy to start a conversation. And yet, that ability to engage an audience, to be *social* with them is what makes brands stand out. It helps them build a relationship with their audience. That, in turn, builds loyalty.

Restaurants are naturally built to be social. Think about it – when your host or hostess walks guests to their seats, he or she is engaging them in conversation, making them feel welcome. When the server greets their new guests, he or she is helping them make a decision about what's best on the menu, another conversation. When the manager comes by to check on the customers, perhaps he or she is sharing the story behind the restaurant, how the owners chose the concept, why they're so passionate about their food.

And yet, most restaurants fail to take this simple social concept and translate it into the digital space. Taking the conversation that happens in the restaurant and doing the same thing on Facebook, Instagram and other social sites eludes most restaurants. That's because it's not as easy as it sounds. It's akin to saying, "just write conversationally, write like you talk." For most people, this takes years of practice.

That's why I suggest you start practicing now. If you can get people talking, responding, and commenting… simply engaging with you on social media, you're going to stand out from the rest of your competitors who simply use the platforms to broadcast. You'll build trust and relationships and get people genuinely excited about coming into your establishment.

Let's get specific about how to do that.

Increase Engagement to Grow Your Facebook Audience

My team and I worked with a popular pizza joint in downtown Las Vegas, ahead of their grand opening. Our goal was to make sure people were talking about the restaurant long before it opened and that on opening night, the line was around the corner to get in.

Before the restaurant even opened, all their social sites were built and optimized, and we started posting a few times a week to give people a "behind the scenes" view as the crew worked to put the final touches on the restaurant. We then used Facebook advertising to promote a contest to win a free private dining experience in connection with the grand opening. Naturally, this created some serious buzz and it helped build page likes and an audience long before opening night.

I mentioned optimization? There's some 101 here that can't be missed. Facebook allows you to provide a LOT of information about your restaurant on its platform. Take advantage of this! Filling out crucial information including your address, hours, menu, and info about your chef is an opportunity that should not be missed. Imagine if someone sees their friend posting about you online. They go to your Facebook page and know exactly what type of food you serve, where you're located and your hours. Boom. They're on their way!

You've also got to make sure your page is active. Back to our downtown pizza joint's grand opening. We used a ton of visuals to get people's attention (No brainer for restaurants, right?). In their case, we built a countdown cover photo that was changed daily. Each day, a new photo would pop up in fans' news feeds "5 more days till we're open!" But we didn't stop with just broadcasting. We engaged fans by asking them what menu item they were most looking forward to. A team member monitored the page regularly and responded to questions about the restaurant. During normal business hours, we acted as the customer service team, responding within an hour.

Growing an audience (especially on Facebook) rarely happens without engagement. You just can't have one without the other. That's why our strategy worked so well. Fans felt a connection to the brand long before the pizza restaurant opened its doors. To this day, it's thriving.

Look for opportunities to engage your audience by taking cues from your customers and your staff. Don't just post a picture of Sunday brunch... add a caption that asks people what they're cooking at home for their Sunday brunch. Then when they respond, add something pithy like: "well, frankly, our French toast sounds much better. We'd be happy to cook for you!" Restaurants have personalities. Make sure yours is shining through on social media. You can promote and engage at the same time. They aren't mutually exclusive.

For many restaurants, especially new establishments, it feels like a heavy lift to start growing a Facebook audience. And in today's crowded landscape, it can be tough to attract new fans on your page. But nothing grows a fan base faster than consistent posting. Let me qualify that... consistent posting that's engaging and interesting to your potential customers. (Add a small paid advertising budget if you're looking for faster results).

Consistent posting can be extremely difficult without a content strategy. I highly recommend making this easy for yourself. For restaurants, the content possibilities are endless... but again, don't forget the personality piece. My team helped several casinos significantly grow their followings (from a thousand fans to more than ten thousand fans in the span of a year). While our content was creative and fun, it also had a specific rhythm to it. We had a growing list of specific content types that acted as our guide.

We got people excited about events. We told people what to expect for Happy Hour. We talked about specific menu items. We shared random food-related quotes. We even introduced people to the staff. Those staff profiles, because they told stories about people, were extremely engaging. I know what you're saying – what about the trolls? Yes, it's a risk to put your employee's photo and some fun info about them out there because people can be mean on social media. That's why we were so focused on the engagement and monitoring piece. We monitored those pages and made sure to delete or ban people if they were saying anything negative about the employees in particular. Side note: it rarely happened. Most people were either happy to see their favorite bartender or entertained by the fun facts about the restaurant's hostess.

Your posting strategy is important, but your networking strategy is paramount. As we discussed before, Facebook's crowded these days and attracting fans is not an easy task. But some of your best promoters are neighboring businesses. If you can forge a relationship with them (in person *and* online), it's a win-win.

For our downtown pizza restaurant, we connected with neighboring businesses on Facebook (by liking their pages and tagging them in appropriate posts). But we went one step further and befriended their social media managers. We offered to share their content – especially around events – and asked them to do the same for us. Talk about word of mouth on steroids.

The restaurant business is interesting because it's difficult to survive in a vacuum. A restaurant is going to have a better chance of survival if it's in a place where there are other thriving restaurants. Working together with those other establishments helps everyone.

Using Facebook Ads & Check-Ins on Facebook

Facebook advertising is a strong play for local restaurants, especially since you can target people within a certain geographical radius. Take the lunch special, for example. Maybe you've got buy one, get one free crab cakes deal. Spend some ad dollars to boost that post to hungry people within a mile or two radius of your restaurant.

If the average lunch cover is worth twenty dollars to you, you can spend twenty dollars to boost that post to people within a mile radius of where you are. If you get four covers as a result of it, that's money well spent. I always caution people about boosting posts, but I think it's perfect for a restaurant. If the restaurant is slow, do a boosted post to try and get some customers in the door. You are already paying your staff to be there so spending a few dollars to draw more customers makes sense. Just make sure you target properly.

Another great visibility driver is check-ins. The only problem with this is it's very server driven. (Read more below on getting your staff engaged in social media). I recommend training your servers to say, "Have you checked in on Facebook? If you do, we'll give you fifteen percent off your check. Just show us the proof on your phone."

Having customers check-in on Facebook is a spectacular way to generate social proof (hey, my friend, Ned, likes that restaurant, maybe I should try it) and to spread the word about your restaurant. When people check-in, you can give them bonus points for posting a picture of their food. There are all kinds of mini-incentives you can use to get other people talking about you, and every little bit helps!

Don't Set it and Forget it

If you're encouraging people to talk about you on Facebook (i.e. check-in, etc.), then you cannot just "set it and forget it." Social media has become an important customer service channel for businesses, especially restaurants. People go to your page to complain about something if they feel they've been wronged. If you're lucky and you've built a raving fan base, some will take the time to post compliments (we can all hope, right?)

Regardless, it's important to respond to people's complaints or concerns quickly. One of the best things to do when someone complains is to respond publicly but then take the conversation private by referring customers to a phone number. That prevents a long drawn-out back & forth in a public forum like Facebook. And it prevents people from simply using your page to vent.

The "don't set it and forget it rule" doesn't just apply to Facebook. Read on...

Be Intentional with Twitter

Twitter is an extraordinarily valuable platform for increasing engagement. We found it especially effective for promoting events. At the pizza joint, we would live tweet events as they were happening. We found it easy to tweet out specials. We would tweet out a lot of the same things that we were doing on Facebook but we found that because we had built a loyal fan following, there was a lot of conversation on Twitter.

For the grand opening, we publicized a specific hashtag and interacted with the people using that hashtag. You don't need a grand opening to create a hashtag specific to your restaurant, though. Choose one and print it out on your table tents or on signage throughout the restaurant. It's a great way to get people talking on your behalf.

We used Twitter for branding and customer service (like if people complained about a long wait). But a lot of what we did with Twitter was personality-driven. We'd tweet out things that reflected the personality of the restaurant, pizza quotes, pictures of food, and other fun content. This type of content works great on the 140-character platform.

We also took advantage of the Twitter search feature. We used Hootsuite so it was easy to set up listening streams. We set up geographical streams so we could see what people were tweeting about nearby. We set up influencer streams. And just like Facebook, we did a lot of Twitter networking with other local businesses, re-tweeting and responding to their content. That's what helped grow the restaurant's following.

The thing about Twitter is, it takes time to do it right. Very few people are willing to put in the time. If you systematize it using a tool like Hootsuite, and if you're intentional about it, Twitter can be a very effective tool for attracting customers and building excitement around your restaurant.

Instagram and Photo Contests

Because food photography needs to be amazing (so your menu items look appetizing when your guests are sharing them on social), many times we toyed with the idea of creating an Instagram Picture Zone within the restaurant. I mean think about it – a section of the restaurant where all the lighting is perfect and when people take pics of their food, their images look like they're professionally done! It could only help your business.

Add some signage with a specific hashtag and you've got a recipe for social success. User generated content with a little bit of control over the quality. Nice.

Take that one step further on Instagram and add a contest to it. Use an app like Woobox to run photo contests, where people can enter by hashtag through Instagram (or Twitter or Facebook). For posting a picture on their page, guests have the potential to win a free dinner. It might encourage them to use your Instagram Photo Zone.

One warning about photo contests, though. They do require people to take several steps to enter. If you're asking them to upload a photo with a certain hashtag there's a little barrier to entry versus just entering their name and email. I think building up a following on Instagram first *then* offering a prize that's worthwhile for people is important. It's not enough to offer a twenty percent off coupon. It's got to be something really special like a free seventy five dollar dinner for two. You have to think about what's going to get people to participate in a contest because the whole goal is to get people posting about you.

For organic posts on Instagram, native photos win every time. And having a photo strategy for your restaurant is crucial. You can do a lot with a smartphone now. It's not like you need a DSLR camera to do all this, but you want to make sure your food looks spectacular. The photo-shopped flyers of your upcoming event are not going to work as well as a picture of your chef in action or one of your servers with a big smile on her face. That kind of authentic content is what you really want to focus on for Instagram. It just performs better.

Instagram advertising is done through Facebook and it is certainly worth considering. The carousel style ads on Facebook or Instagram are great because your ad viewers could just swipe through different dishes from the restaurant. If you do it right and you know your target customers, something will peak their interest.

Video on Social Media

There is so much visual content in a restaurant atmosphere that using video is a natural fit. If your executive chef has any sort of cache or celebrity status, then Facebook live can be great tool. You could have your executive chef showing people on Facebook Live how to create the meal of the day. Facebook loves live video and they'll reward you by showing it to more people in the newsfeed.

Not everyone is comfortable doing live video though. There are other things you can do with visual content. You can post lightly edited video from events, a highlight reel of sorts. I also love the idea of an introduction from the proprietor, chef, or a server that says, "Welcome in, when you come here, this is how we want you to feel." I think that type of thing makes your posts warm and inviting.

Or maybe you have raving fans who are regulars. Get them to talk to the camera about what they love best about your restaurant, even showing off some of their favorite meals. It's likely they'll share their post with their friends, bringing you even more exposure.

Just a quick tip on making sure your video reaches more people: for each of the social media sites, video uploaded directly to that platform will perform better than sharing a *link* to a YouTube video (especially on Facebook). So if you create a video and post it on YouTube, also post the full video file to Facebook or Instagram or Twitter, not just the YouTube link.

On your website, YouTube can be used for the video hosting for a website, but it is also important for search engine optimization (SEO). Google owns YouTube and

SOCIAL MEDIA MARKETING FOR RESTAURANTS

YouTube is the second most searched site behind Google. So making sure your video lives on YouTube is very important and that's it's optimized so people find it!

If I'm going to take the time to create a video for my restaurant, I'm probably going to choose Facebook video first. Not necessarily live, but I might record a video on my phone and upload it to the restaurant's Facebook page. Go one step further and put some ad money behind that video. Video ads are some of the top performers on Facebook. And if you want to get attention for your restaurant, nothing beats video.

Reviews

Want to take control of your online reputation? Then you need to make sure you've optimized your presence on Yelp AND that you have a plan in place to manage that platform. Yelp is the first place potential customers are going to go to find out what others are saying about you, and it's the first place dissatisfied customers are going to go to complain.

This is where you've got to be proactive. It's important to have a review monitoring system in place so you know when someone's talking about you *and* a plan to manage and respond to reviews. People put plenty of stock in online reviews. I think they put even more stock in them when it comes to restaurants. It's not uncommon for people to read reviews on multiple review sites before choosing a restaurant.

On the proactive side of things, you should actively be seeking new reviews. Train your front of the house staff to ask for them. At the end of a customer's experience when the check is delivered, have your servers ask if the customer was happy with their experience. If the answer is yes, the server should solicit a review. Make this as easy as possible. Table signage that explains how to post a review is helpful. Putting your review funnel's URL on the receipt is also great.

The bottom line is, we, as humans, respond more favorably when asked personally to do something. If they're asked by a server, your customers are more likely to take the time to post a positive review.

Getting Your Staff Involved in the Social Media Process

Enlisting the help of staff to generate reviews is a great way to get them involved in the social media process. But it shouldn't stop there.

While I highly recommend that restaurants (like any other business) should have guidelines for social media use by employees, they should also find a way to enlist their staff to amplify their social media presence.

Here are just a couple ideas: set up an in-house competition – the person who generates the most reviews in a month gets a gift card. Or the server who shares the most posts on their personal social media gets 2 hours off. Or the hostess who encourages the most customer check-ins gets a valuable prize. Do something to get everyone involved and excited about your social media presence.

Many restaurants don't have the budget to hire a social media manager. In that case, appoint a social media "captain" for each shift. The captain monitors what's being said on social media (at reasonable intervals). And he/she looks for opportunities to engage or triage (if needed).

Think about how powerful it would be if you (the customer) are sitting at your table and you tweet, "This was the worst service I've had in the last couple of years." Within five minutes, somebody from the staff comes over and says, "We're really sorry you didn't have a great experience here. What could we have done to make things better?" You'll likely win back a customer who otherwise would've been lost.

I've shared a ton of ideas you can implement to really make social media the main marketing driver for your restaurant. It works. I've seen it first-hand. I do realize that many of you reading this may not have the staff or budget to go "all-in" like this on social media. I'd encourage you, then, to focus on one thing only: remembering the power of social media as a *social* platform, a place where you can start relationships with potential customers long before they set foot in your restaurant. By using a conversational tone, showing off your restaurant's personality online, and engaging with your audience, you'll be one step ahead of your competitors who are solely focused on broadcasting. Good luck!

14 CONCLUSION

Social media marketing for restaurants can be very powerful but it is important to start with strategy, and to develop a content calendar based on the platforms that make the most sense for the restaurant. It is important to have a social media plan/policy that addresses:

- who your current and ideal customers are
- what social media channels will be used
- what the type and tone of posts will be
- what should not be posted and language to avoid
- schedule of the posts by platform
- who can / will post

Having a well thought out strategy drives more effective results and makes it easier to execute social media marketing. This is a key step many restaurants skip.

Social media marketing is still underused or misused by too many restaurants. Restaurants are an industry that fits perfectly with social media. People are naturally social about food, so having a plan to get user generated content and to drive quality reviews can make a big impact. Restaurants need to ask your customers their customers to post reviews and make it as easy as possible for them to do so.

I wrote this book because I think social media marketing offers restaurants a very cost effective marketing solution. When users share content about your restaurant it gets so much more exposure and reach than many of the posts that come directly from your restaurant. When a restaurant develops an engaged audience on social media, some serious amplification of reach can occur. This makes social media a powerful channel.

At the same time, because of the potential and viral possibility of social media, it is critically important for restaurants to monitor and respond to comments and posts about the restaurant. Not playing attention to what people are saying on social media is at best a missed opportunity to deepen a relationship with a customer, and at worst, it can be catastrophic when negative comments are not addressed.

Social media can be used for free and it also offers some fairly low cost and highly targeted advertising opportunities. But just because social media can be free, that doesn't mean that are no costs. It is important to factor in time to plan, train staff members, and execute social media marketing.

I think that social media advertising, especially for a business like a restaurant, provides a really great opportunity to use the information that people are disclosing on social networks to target ads to reach of exactly the right people. All social media platforms offer the ability to create ads. I believe Facebook, Instagram and Snapchat provide the greatest advertising opportunities for restaurants depending on who their ideal customers are.

Another key take away is that restaurant owners need to realize that social media done in a vacuum is not going to be very effective. You really need to organize it in terms of a campaign with a well thought-out strategy. If you're going to run a Facebook contest, it takes more than just setting up an app like WooBox on your Facebook page and hoping that people register for your contest and like your Facebook page. You have to do work to drive them to the contest.

To promote a contest you might have to do a Facebook ad, put something on your website, tweet about it, post signage in your restaurant, and so on, to make sure people know about the contest. You have to drive traffic and use a multi-touch strategy.

It's really important to know who your current and target customers are. Not defining them makes it really difficult to find the most effective way to use social media.

Social media marketing is not particularly difficult; it's just that many restaurants don't know what capabilities each of the social media platforms has. My goal is to help restaurants recognize what's possible with tools that are free or nearly free and to leverage some of the cheapest advertising strategies available.

There are several social media platforms that can be used effectively by most restaurants. Facebook is an obvious choice. But I think there are tremendous opportunities to use Instagram and Snapchat. Google and Yelp reviews are extremely important, so having a review funnel and process to drive reviews is critical. The other platforms offer some great options to consider.

The power of social proof is extremely important for a restaurant. Each restaurant, whether it is independently owned or a part of a franchise, has to have a strategy in place to let each location effectively use social media and create and manage a review funnel. If not, those restaurants are missing out on one of the most powerful and cost effective marketing solutions available. In my opinion, each restaurant has to have some level of local control of their social media marketing.

ABOUT THE AUTHORS

Ken Tucker
Founder, Changescape Web

www.changescapeweb.com

ken@changescapeweb.com

Ken Tucker is the founder of Changescape Web (www.changescapeweb.com), a Small Business Marketing and Website Design Agency. Changescape Web specializes in developing comprehensive integrated marketing strategy and campaigns for small and mid-sized businesses across the Midwest.

Ken is a Master Duct Tape Marketing Certified Consultant (since 2015) and an Inbound Marketing Certified Professional (since 2010). He serves as the chief marketing strategist for Changescape Web, which he founded in 2005.

He also provides training in the Duct Tape Marketing System and Social Media as well as offering a complete range of website design, search engine optimization, lead generation, and marketing strategy services.

He taught Social Media Marketing and Content Management Systems at the St. Charles Community College for 5 years (from 2011 – 2016).

Ken currently serves as Co-Chair of the St. Charles County Chambers of Commerce Technology Committee and served on the Board of Directors for the Greater St. Charles County Chamber and the Cottleville-Weldon Spring Chamber. He speaks to chambers and business organizations on topics such as marketing strategy, online marketing, social media marketing, and local search engine optimization.

Follow Ken Tucker:
www.twitter.com/changescape
www.linkedin.com/in/kentuckerweb
www.plus.google.com/+Changescapeweb

Special Offers from Ken:
Changescape Web Can Help Your Restaurant's Social Media effectiveness. Do you wonder how your restaurant is doing against competitors on social media?

We offer a complimentary Social Media review for your restaurant as well against 3 competitors. We'll also include a reputation report for you.

Visit http://changescapeweb.com/social-media-review-report/ and complete the information in the form. We will create the report and scheduled a time with you to review your results.

Ken is available to your organization to speak on a variety of topics related to Marketing Systems, Social Media, Inbound Marketing and Online Marketing. Visit our website to learn more and to book Ken as a speaker at http://changescapeweb.com/professional-speakers/

Nina Radetich
Founder, Radetich Marketing +
Media

www.ninaradetich.com

nina@ninaradetich.com

Nina Radetich is the founder of Radetich Marketing + Media, a Las Vegas-based marketing agency dedicated to creating quality content that generates results. Nina is a Duct Tape Marketing Certified Consultant with a deep background in journalism.

Nina always dreamed of owning her own business and took the plunge into entrepreneurship in 2012. Her agency has helped countless businesses grow – from wellness experts to lawyers to wealth advisors to restaurants to casinos.

Her journalism background was integral in her agency's efforts to create successful social media marketing campaigns for local restaurants, including the launch of a popular gourmet pizza joint with a celebrity chef.

In what Nina likes to call her "old life," she spent close to two decades as a television news anchor on both the NBC and ABC affiliates in Las Vegas. She covered several memorable stories in that time, winning an Emmy and an Edward R. Murrow along the way. She remains very involved in her local community, acting as the emcee for an annual event honoring law enforcement, and serving on the Advisory Council for Spread the Word Nevada, a charity promoting literacy for underprivileged kids.

Because of her background, Nina loves to help clients think outside the box when it comes to content. She specializes in video strategies for small businesses. From podcasting to livestreaming, Nina helps businesses see the potential of audio/visual content and create a plan for solid execution.

Follow Nina:
www.twitter.com/NinaRVegas
www.facebook.com/NinaRadetich
www.linkedin.com/in/NinaRadetich
www.instagram.com/NinaRadetich

Special Offers from Nina:

Are you ready to amplify the buzz about your restaurant? We can help you add video and audio content to your marketing mix. Book a free 15 minute video strategy session with us. Just go here to find out if you qualify https://ninaradetich.com/video-strategy-session/

Made in the USA
Middletown, DE
13 December 2020